"Chris Morphew is like Tim Keller for teens. In this short book, he tackles some of today's tough questions with Scripture, wisdom and clarity—and just the right amount of fun to keep young readers turning the page. I cannot wait to put this book into the hands of my three children."

CHAMP THORNTON, Pastor; Author, *The Radical Book for Kids* and *Why Do We Say Good Night?*

"Chris Morphew has given families such a gift with *How Do We Know That Christianity Is Really True?* As I read it with my 13- and 10-year-old children, we laughed at his stories, discussed the questions that came up, and learned things we didn't know before. I watched as their faith was strengthened and their heart for the lost grew. I highly recommend this book to parents, youth and children's leaders, and Christian schools. We look forward to reading the other books in the series."

CATHERINE PARKS, Author, *Empowered* and *Strong*

"I've loved reading through *How Do We Know That Christianity Is Really True?* with my 10- and 13-year-old children. What a rare combination—taking seriously our children's real faith questions while also offering engaging, brief chapters. This book is a gift for parents as our children ask great questions, which we can work through together in these pages."

ED DREW, Director, Faith in Kids; Author, *Meals With Jesus*

"What an excellent series—seriously excellent! I am certain Chris Morphew's chatty style, clear explanations, relevant illustrations and personal insights will engage, inform and equip tweens as they work through some of the big questions they and their peers will be asking."

TAMAR POLLARD, Director for Families, Children and Youth Ministry, Grace Community Church, Bedford

"Chris has a knack for making complicated things simpler, making confusing things make sense, and making everything fun. He takes your questions—and you—seriously and knows where you can find real, honest-to-God answers."

DR NATASHA MOORE, Research Fellow, Centre for Public Christianity

"Questions and doubts aren't bad at all. Chris Morphew gives us big truths in simple and clear words to help us grow. Pick this book up, follow the evidence and see where it leads. "

BARBARA REAOCH, Former Director, Children's Division, Bible Study Fellowship; Author, *A Jesus Christmas*

"Maybe you've been singing songs about God, Jesus and the Bible since you were little. And maybe, over the years, you've had questions about whether the things you've been taught about Christianity are actually true. Or perhaps you're hearing about Jesus for the first time, and you have questions about that too. Well, I think you're going to love spending time with Chris Morphew in this book as together you dig up solid, helpful, satisfying answers to lots of questions—including some you didn't even know."

COLIN BUCHANAN, Singer/Songwriter

HOW DO WE KNOW that Christianity IS REALLY TRUE?

CHRIS MORPHEW

Illustrated by Emma Randall

thegoodbook COMPANY

To John Dickson,
For helping me see the truth about
Jesus more clearly.

How Do We Know That Christianity Is Really True?

Published by:
The Good Book Company

thegoodbook COMPANY

thegoodbook.com | thegoodbook.co.uk
thegoodbook.com.au | thegoodbook.co.nz | thegoodbook.co.in

ISBN: 9781784986148 | Printed in the UK

Illustrated by Emma Randall | Design by André Parker

Contents

Chapter 1

THE TWO MOST IMPORTANT QUESTIONS

All across the world today, millions of people are living their whole lives based on a claim from ancient history that, when you think about it, is kind of hard to believe.

They say that, around 2,000 years ago, a man named Jesus of Nazareth was arrested and sentenced to death. He was dragged outside the city of Jerusalem in Israel and nailed to a cross. Jesus died and was buried.

That's not the part that's hard to believe, though. After all, everyone dies at some point.

It's the *next* part that might sound ridiculous.

See, these millions of people are convinced that, a few days after his burial, Jesus came back to life again. They believe that a few weeks after that he returned, alive, to heaven—and that he's still alive today.

On the other hand, all across the world today, there are plenty of *other* people who think the idea of a person rising from the dead is absolute nonsense.

Some of them think that Jesus didn't exist at all. Others think he probably *did* exist but that he was just an ordinary human being with some nice things to say about loving one another—an ordinary human being who died and then *stayed* dead.

So who's right? Did Jesus *actually* come back to life, or didn't he?

The reason I ask is that I'm convinced that answering *this* question is the surest way to figure out if Christianity is worth taking seriously.

But first... I wonder how you've ended up holding this book.

Maybe your family thinks Jesus is a big deal, and so far you've just kind of gone along with that, but now you're starting to ask yourself if you can *really* trust that Christianity is true.

Or maybe you've made the decision to follow Jesus for yourself, but your friends or your family think he's a fairytale, and you're beginning to worry that they might be right. Or maybe they follow a different religion completely, and now you don't know *what* to believe.

Or maybe *you're* the one who thinks Jesus is a fairytale, but someone's given you this book because they're trying to convince you that he's worth taking seriously after all.

Or maybe you're somewhere in the middle. Maybe you've got a sneaking suspicion that Jesus might be who the Bible says he is, but you want to know if there's any solid evidence.

However you've come to have this book, I'm so glad you're here, because it turns out there really *is* solid evidence that Christianity is true—and like I said, it all comes down to one question:

Did Jesus really come back to life?

In fact, I'm convinced that this is the second-most-important question anyone can ever ask.

(Oh, and don't worry—by the end of this book, we'll get to the *most* important question too.)

△ △△△ △△△△ △

Why does it matter so much whether Jesus rose from the dead?

Because the world is *full* of great teachers and leaders saying, "Here's the way to find God", or "Here's the truth about the world", or "Here's how you can have the life you've always wanted"—but Jesus said something completely different.

Jesus didn't say, "Here is the way", or "Here is the truth", or "Here is the life".

He said, "I *am* the way and the truth and the life" (John 14 v 6).

Jesus claimed to be God himself, the one true King of the universe who made us and loves us.

Jesus claimed that every single human being who has ever lived has made a mess of their relationship with God and that we need *him* to come and rescue us.

Jesus claimed that by dying on the cross, he was healing our broken relationships with God.

Jesus claimed that if we put our trust in him instead of trusting in our own efforts or goodness, we can have life with him—life to the full, here and now, and perfect life forever with him when he returns to heal God's broken world and make it our perfect home again.

And here's the thing: if Jesus really *did* come back to life, *those aren't just claims*.

They're *true*.

If Jesus' resurrection is real, it's all the proof we need that he really is who he says he is—because only God himself has that kind of power.

Of course, on the other hand, if Jesus *didn't* come back to life, he was either lying or crazy or both—and we shouldn't listen to a word he said.

If Jesus *didn't* come back to life, all of those millions of Christians are wasting their lives following a dead man.

Or, as one of the Bible writers put it: "If Christ [Jesus] has not been raised, our preaching is useless and so is your faith" (1 Corinthians 15 v 14).

This is why the question of whether Jesus rose from the dead is such a big deal—because there's no third option in the middle. If Jesus came back to life, he's the King of the universe and *everyone* should follow him—but if Jesus *didn't* come back to life, it's all a bunch of garbage and *no one* should follow him.

△ △ △ △ △ △ △ △ △

So how do we figure out whether to believe in Jesus' resurrection?

Well, some people say it's basically a choice between *evidence* and *faith*.

They say people who believe in gravity or climate change or the Big Bang are relying on *evidence*—on solid facts and information and research.

And they say that people who believe in God and the Bible and all that stuff are relying on *faith*—that they're choosing to *ignore* the facts and information and research, and believe in something else instead.

According to this way of looking at things, *evidence* and *faith* are basically opposites—the more *evidence* you have, the less faith you need; the more *faith* you have, the less you care about having any actual evidence.

This is a *really* common way of thinking about evidence and faith, and it's what most people assume the Bible means when it talks about having *faith* in Jesus' resurrection.

But this is *not* how the Bible describes faith at all!

In the Bible, faith means *being convinced by the evidence*. So when the Bible talks about putting your *faith* in Jesus, it's not talking about believing in him *without* any evidence; it's talking about believing in him *because* of the evidence.

△△△△△△△△△

Here's a different example to explain what I mean.

I have faith in my parents. I have faith that they love me and want what's best for me. And that faith didn't just come out of nowhere. It's based on years and years of evidence.

It's based on all the time they've spent feeding me, and clothing me and taking care of me. It's based on all the times they've *told* me they love me, and all the times they've *shown* me their love through their actions.

Because of all that evidence, I have faith in my parents' love for me.

Now, I could be wrong.

My parents might not love me at all.

Maybe they've just been *pretending* to love me for the past 35 years. Maybe they're not even my real parents. Maybe they're aliens from a distant galaxy dressed in really convincing human suits.

It's possible. But it would be pretty ridiculous for me to assume that was true—because there's a *ton* of evidence for the "my parents love me" theory, and *zero* evidence for the "my parents are aliens" theory.

When I look at all the evidence, the *most reasonable conclusion* is that those two people living in my parents' apartment are my *actual human parents who really do love me*—and so that's the truth I put my faith in.

Now, if I suddenly uncover a whole bunch of *new* evidence—if I find a laser blaster under my parents' couch, and a spaceship in their garage, and a pile of dirty human suits in their laundry basket—then I'm going to need to go back and reconsider my beliefs a bit.

But in the meantime, I'm going to go right on assuming my parents are real human beings who really do love me.

△△△△△△△△△

This is exactly how we need to treat the resurrection of Jesus: we need to follow the evidence and see where it leads.

And the good news is, because the Bible makes *historical* claims about Jesus, we can use the tools of historical investigation to help us figure out if those claims are true.

That's what we're going to do in this book.

First, we'll ask the question, *Can we trust what the Bible says about Jesus?*

There are a bunch of tests that historians use to figure out how much they can trust an ancient document. We're going to put the Bible through some of those tests and see how trustworthy it actually is.

Now, as a follower of Jesus, I believe that the Bible is *so much more* than just another set of ancient writings. I believe it's God's word and that everything it tells us is absolutely trustworthy and true.

But for the next few chapters, I'm going to put all that aside. I'm not going to be exploring what *Christians* believe about Jesus. I'm going to be outlining what *historians* generally agree about Jesus whether they're Christians or not.

Once we've done that, we'll move on to our next question: *Can we trust that Jesus rose from the dead?* Because, like I said, I'm convinced it's the second-most-important question anyone can ever ask—the question the whole Christian faith depends on. And then, once you've decided on your answer to that question, you'll be ready for the most important question of all: *If Jesus really did come back to life... what am I going to do about it?*

Because if the resurrection is true, it's not just some amazing thing that happened, way back in the past. It has the power to completely transform your life today.

If the resurrection is true, it changes everything.

Chapter 2

HOW MUCH DO WE REALLY KNOW ABOUT JESUS?

Imagine I walk into the playground at the school where I work one morning after a day off sick, and a five-year-old kid races up to me and says, "Mr Morphew, did you hear about the tiger that was running through the school yesterday?"

Should I just *believe* them?

Well, probably not. An escaped tiger running through my school is a pretty unusual event—and so maybe this kid's just making it up, or maybe they're passing on a weird rumour that someone *else* made up.

But let's say this kid's friends all back the story up: "It's true, Mr Morphew! We saw it too!"

Now should I believe them?

Again, probably not. Because how do I know this isn't just some weird prank they've planned together?

But then let's say I continue through the playground, and I overhear a dad telling his daughter, "You'll be *fine*. They caught the tiger last night. It's back in the zoo where it belongs."

That changes things a bit, right? Because now I have at least *two* different sources of information about this tiger. And they're *independent* sources—I can be pretty sure they didn't get their information by copying each other.

And *then* let's say I sit down to check my email, and there's a message from the principal sitting in my inbox:

> *ATTENTION ALL STAFF—PLEASE MEET IN THE STAFF ROOM AT 8.00 AM FOR AN UPDATE ON YESTERDAY'S TIGER INCIDENT.*

Suddenly, this escaped tiger story seems a whole lot more likely to be true, right? Because now I have a *third* independent source. And the more independent sources of information I have about an event—even a really unusual event—the more confident I can be that the event actually happened.

△△△△△△△△△

Historians use this same strategy to investigate people and events from ancient history. Asking, "How many independent sources of information do we have?" is a useful way of figuring out how confident we can be that a claim about history is trustworthy.

And so let's focus that question in on Jesus. You might

think the only reason we know about Jesus at all is because he shows up in the Bible—but that's actually not true. So to start our investigation, let's look at what historical sources *outside* the Bible can tell us about Jesus.

First up, we have a Roman historian named Tacitus, who was born less than 30 years after Jesus died, when many of the people who actually met Jesus were still alive. Tacitus wrote a history of the Roman Empire called the *Annals*. It only gives Jesus a short mention, but it's enough to tell us a few things:

- Jesus lived during the time when Tiberius Caesar was emperor of Rome.
- Jesus was sentenced to death by Pontius Pilate, the Roman governor of the region of Judea.
- For some reason, decades after Jesus' death, people were still following him.

Obviously that's not tons of information, but it's a start.

Next, we have a Jewish historian named Josephus, born less than *ten* years after Jesus died. He wrote a history of the Jewish people called *Jewish Antiquities*, which gives us a few more details:

- Jesus was a wise teacher.
- Jesus became known for doing "surprising deeds" (aka miracles).

- Jesus had a brother named James, who was also put to death.
- People called Jesus the "Christ" (a title which means "the chosen one" or "King").

Like Tacitus, Josephus also mentions that Pontius Pilate was the one who had Jesus killed. But Josephus gives us the extra detail that Jesus died by *crucifixion*—by being nailed to a cross. And, like Tacitus, Josephus also confirms the strange detail that Jesus' followers *kept* following him, even after he died.

Our third independent source is a Roman governor named Pliny the Younger, who lived at around the same time as Tacitus and Josephus. From a letter that Pliny wrote to the Roman Emperor Trajan, we pick up an extra little detail about the early Christians singing songs to Jesus as if he were a god.

There are also a handful of other mentions of Jesus in other ancient documents, but here's the point: we don't need the Bible in order to know that Jesus is a real person from history.

In fact, here's what we can piece together about Jesus without even opening a Bible:

> *Jesus was a real human being with a brother named James, who lived in Israel while Tiberius Caesar was emperor of Rome and Pontius Pilate was governor of Judea. Jesus had a reputation for being a wise teacher*

and a performer of miracles, and some people called him the "Christ", claiming he was a king.

Jesus was arrested in Jerusalem at around the time of the Jewish Passover festival. On the orders of Pontius Pilate, he was nailed to a cross and killed. But then, after Jesus' death, reports spread that he had come back to life and showed himself to his followers. As a result, people not only kept following Jesus, they worshipped him—and instead of shrinking, the number of Jesus' followers grew and grew.

Of course, when we *do* open the Bible, we find even more sources of information about Jesus—but before we do that, I probably need to clear something up.

Right now, you might be thinking, "Hang on a minute! The Bible is a *religious* book, not a *history* book! You can't trust the Bible writers' descriptions of Jesus—they're totally biased! They're just trying to convince you to believe in him!"

And it's true: the Bible *is* biased.

But, as any good historian will tell you, so is *every other historical text.*

Tacitus, for example, was biased *against* Jesus. He called Christianity a dangerous superstition! But that doesn't mean historians just *ignore* what he wrote about Jesus.

And the people who wrote about Jesus in the Bible were biased *towards* Jesus—but historians don't just ignore what *they* wrote about him either.

Good historians realise that *every* text is written by a particular person with a particular point of view—and so if you were going to ignore every historical source with any kind of bias, you'd have to throw out pretty much *everything*.

So instead, what good historians do is try to *understand* each writer's point of view, and keep it in mind while they're reading—which means that while historians might not treat the Bible as *more* reliable than other historical sources, they don't treat it as *less* reliable either.

△△△△△△△△△

The other thing to remember about the Bible is that it's not just *one* book. It's a whole library of different books by different authors. And so when we open up the Bible, we don't find just *one* source on Jesus; we find a whole bunch of accounts written by different people.

Figuring out exactly how many of these sources were *independent* gets a bit more complicated and technical than we have time for here—but the short version is that historians agree the New Testament of the Bible contains *at least* five independent sources of information on Jesus, and probably a couple more than that.

And when we add those to the ten or so independent sources from *outside* the Bible, that gives us a total of at least 15 independent sources of information about Jesus.

That might not seem like a huge number—until you realise that for plenty of important people from ancient history, we only have *one* or *two* sources. By ancient history standards, 15 independent sources is *heaps*!

If I had *15* different people giving me information about a tiger running loose in my school, and if I knew that none of them had talked to each other about it before they talked to me, I'd have more than enough reason to start taking that tiger story seriously.

And with 15 independent sources all giving us information about Jesus, we have more than enough reason to take *his* story seriously too.

Chapter 3

WHEN WERE OUR SOURCES ABOUT JESUS written?

Almost 2,000 years ago, in the year AD 70, the Roman general Titus and his army surrounded the city of Jerusalem. They broke through the city walls, took over the city and set fire to the enormous temple building.

If you visit Jerusalem today, you can walk down a section of the old main street, smashed and broken, with giant chunks of what used to be the temple wall lying in massive piles on the ground.

Let's say you wanted to learn some more about these events. What do you think would be your best source of information?

a) A book by the Jewish historian Josephus, who was working as a translator for Titus at the time and saw these events happen.

b) The diary of a soldier who visited Jerusalem around 1,000 years after the events.

c) A postcard written by a tourist who visited Jerusalem last year, nearly 2,000 years after the events.

If you asked any good historian, they'd tell you to go with Josephus.

All three of these people visited Jerusalem, but Josephus was an eyewitness—he saw it all happen—and his book, *The Jewish War*, was written only a few years after the Romans smashed their way into Jerusalem.

And in general, the *earlier* the source—the closer it is to the original events—the more likely that source is to give us accurate information about those events.

So what about our sources on Jesus in the Bible? Are they early enough to be reliable?

The New Testament of the Bible is made up of 27 books and letters about Jesus. The *earliest* of these sources was written within about 20 years of Jesus' death. Our first complete biography of Jesus (the Gospel of Mark) was written within 40 years. And the *latest* biography (the Gospel of John) was written within about 70 years.

In other words, the New Testament was being written while many of the original eyewitnesses—the people who actually *met* Jesus—were still alive.

70 years might still seem like a long time—until you realise that, for plenty of other important people from ancient

history, our best sources don't show up until *hundreds* of years after they died. By ancient history standards, our New Testament sources on Jesus are really early.

Even so, this doesn't mean people weren't already writing and talking about Jesus' life, death and resurrection way earlier than that. In fact, inside our New Testament sources, we find evidence of even *earlier* sources of information about Jesus.

For example, look at the way Luke introduces his biography of Jesus:

> *Many have undertaken to draw up an account of the things that have been fulfilled among us, just as they were handed down to us by those who from the first were eyewitnesses and servants of the word. With this in mind, since I myself have carefully investigated everything from the beginning, I too decided to write an orderly account for you, most excellent Theophilus, so that you may know the certainty of the things you have been taught. (Luke 1 v 1-4)*

Luke wrote his Gospel within 50 years of Jesus' death, to help a man named Theophilus understand the truth of what he'd already heard about Jesus.

But notice how Luke says that, before he wrote his book, many other people had *already* put together accounts of Jesus' life and teaching. Luke says he used these *earlier* sources, dating back to the original eyewitnesses, to help him write his book.

Historians agree that one of these ancient sources was Mark (who, like we said before, wrote his Gospel about a decade earlier). But as they study Luke's writing, they also see evidence that he borrowed chunks of writing from two other key sources, both likely written a decade or two earlier than Mark's Gospel.

We don't have *full* copies of those earlier sources anymore—but thankfully, we've still got the bits Luke borrowed to use in his book.

△△△△△△△△△

But at this point, people often raise another question: how do we know that what we read in our modern Bibles is the same information Jesus' first followers originally wrote down?

We don't have the original handwritten versions of any of the New Testament texts. What we do have are ancient *copies* of the originals—and so how do we know those copies are accurate? How do we know our sources on Jesus haven't been changed over time, either accidentally or on purpose?

This is where the *number* of ancient copies becomes really important. Because if I only have *two* copies of some bit of the New Testament, and they're both different from each other, how could I possibly know which copy matches the original and which one has been changed? How do I even know that *either* of them match the original?

But let's say I have *20* ancient copies. And let's say 18 of those copies all match each other, but the other two contain some little bits that don't match.

Well, as any historian will tell you, that would be like winning the lottery! Because at that point, it's pretty safe to assume that those 18 matching texts also match the *original* text, and that the non-matching bits in the other two copies are errors that have crept in somewhere along the way.

Here's the thing though: we don't have 20 ancient New Testament manuscripts.

We have *thousands*—way more than any other text in ancient history!

When historians compare these ancient copies to each other, they find that the texts are 99.5% identical—and with so many copies to compare, they can confidently work out where any little changes have crept in to a particular copy.

All of which means we can absolutely trust that we're reading the *same* historical claims those first followers of Jesus wrote down nearly 2,000 years ago.

△ △△△ △△△△△

All of this is a big deal in our search for the truth about Jesus' resurrection—because it shows us that, right from the beginning, Jesus' followers were *already* claiming he had come back to life.

The reason this matters is that some people want to say the resurrection is a *myth* that developed over time.

The theory goes like this: "Jesus' first followers never *actually* saw Jesus alive again after he died. But they still had his teachings, and all these great memories of Jesus, and as they thought about all that, it was like he was *alive again in their hearts*, even though he was actually still dead. But then, over time, as these stories got passed down through the years, they got all muddled and were transformed into this myth about Jesus *actually* coming back to life, even though it had never really happened."

The problem with this theory is that it completely contradicts all of our actual historical evidence!

No serious historian puts Jesus' resurrection in the "myth" category, because myths like this take *generations* to develop—and we have solid written evidence dating back to within just a few years of Jesus' death that his disciples were already worshipping Jesus as their risen King.

Whatever Jesus' resurrection is, it *can't* be a myth. There just wasn't enough time for it to develop.

Right from the *very* beginning, Jesus' first followers claimed that Jesus had really, truly risen from the dead and appeared to them.

Which leads us to the next obvious question: Were they telling the truth?

Chapter 4

HOW DO WE KNOW JESUS' followers didn't just MAKE IT ALL UP?

Time for another multiple choice question. Let's say I want to apply for a job as head chef at a fancy restaurant. I've never worked as a chef before, but I *really* want this job, so I decide to just make up a bunch of stuff for the application form. Which lies am I more likely to tell?

a) That I've spent years working for the fanciest restaurants in Paris and New York, that I've been trained by the best chefs in the business, and that I've won tons of awards for my incredible cooking.

b) That I've been fired from every restaurant I've ever worked at, that I only know how to cook two-minute noodles, and that I'm clumsy and dirty and one time I accidentally burned down my whole kitchen.

Obviously I'd choose Option A, right? If I'm going to lie to get this job, I'm at least going to pick lies that make me look *good*, not ones that make me look like a total embarrassment!

In the last chapter, we saw that we've got solid historical evidence that, right from the beginning, Jesus' disciples were claiming he had risen from the dead.

But how do we know they didn't just make it all up?

What if Jesus' first followers *invented* the stories of Jesus' resurrection and all his other miracles, just so they could gather a bunch of followers, start up a religion and put themselves in charge?

It might sound like a pretty good theory, but here's one of the biggest problems with it: if Jesus' disciples were going to lie about Jesus, surely they'd invent stories that made them look *good*, right?

But when you read the biographies of Jesus, that's not what you find. Instead, you find story after story that makes Jesus' first followers look like total embarrassments.

Jesus is repeatedly *amazed* by how slow his disciples are to understand what he's trying to teach them (Mark 7 v 18). He says it's like they're blind and deaf (Mark 8 v 18). When Jesus tells stories to explain who he is, his disciples don't get what he's talking about (Mark 4 v 13). When they're in danger, they freak out instead of trusting Jesus to help them (Mark 4 v 40). They seem to keep on forgetting his power, even though he shows it to them again and again

(Mark 8 v 19-21)—and when they *do* remember, they ask if they can use it to do violence (Luke 9 v 54).

When Jesus first announces his plan to save humanity by dying and rising again, his friend Peter tries to talk him out of it (Mark 8 v 31-32). And no matter how many times Jesus tries to explain that this is *the whole reason he came*, his disciples *still* don't get it (Mark 9 v 30-32, 10 v 32-34).

On the night before Jesus is nailed to the cross, his disciples all swear they'll *never* abandon him (Mark 14 v 31), but when Jesus invites them to stay up with him while he prays, they all fall asleep—*three times* (v 32-41). Then, when Jesus is arrested, they all run away and abandon him (v 50). One of them is so desperate to get out of there that, when the guards grab his clothes he shrugs them off and runs away naked (v 51-52). That same night, Peter, who just swore he'd rather *die* than leave Jesus (v 31), pretends three times that he doesn't even *know* him (v 66-72).

All of which leads to a question: if Jesus' disciples were going to *make up* biographies of Jesus, do you really think they'd include all *that*?

△△△△△△△△△

And that's before we even get to the cross.

If you're familiar with the story of Jesus, the fact that he died on a cross probably isn't a shock to you—but that's only because the world's had 2,000 years to get used to the idea.

Back in the first century, the idea that someone who died on a cross could be any kind of saviour or king was *ridiculous*. Death by crucifixion was the most awful, embarrassing, shameful punishment imaginable. Not to mention the obvious fact that crucified people ended up *dead*—and who wants to devote their life to following a dead man?

The writers of the Bible *knew* how crazy their story sounded to the people around them. In one of his letters, Paul admitted that the idea of Jesus saving the world by dying on the cross sounded like "foolishness" (1 Corinthians 1 v 18).

Jesus' own people, the Israelites, were expecting God to send them a rescuing king—but the idea of that king dying on the cross sounded *nuts*, because why on earth would God let his Chosen One be brutally murdered?

And to people living *outside* of Israel, the idea of a crucified saviour seemed just as ridiculous.

If you visit the Palatine Hill Museum in Rome, you can see a piece of ancient graffiti, mocking a man named Alexamenos for following Jesus. It's a picture of Jesus on the cross, but instead of a human head, he's got the head of a donkey. Beside the cross stands a man raising his hand in worship. Underneath, the artist has scratched the caption, "Alexamenos worships his god". Whoever drew it clearly thought Alexamenos was pretty stupid for worshipping someone who was crucified.

As we've seen already, there's solid evidence from both inside and outside the Bible that Jesus really did get put to death on a cross—but *another* great reason to trust that it's true is how completely embarrassing it is.

If Jesus' followers were going to *make up* a story, it's hard to imagine why they would have made it up like this.

Which brings us to the resurrection.

If the biographies of Jesus are made up, this is the biggest lie of all. Sure, people living back then might have known less about science than we do, but they knew perfectly well that dead people usually stayed dead.

Which is why it's so weird that all four biographies of Jesus in the Bible include a detail that, if anything, seems to make the resurrection *harder* to believe—or at least, the original writers and readers would have thought so. They say that the first people to see Jesus alive were *women*.

Here's the thing: back in those days, Israel's law said that only *men* could give evidence in court; women weren't allowed.

Why? Because the men in charge had decided that, in scary or dangerous situations, women were too *emotional* to be trusted.

Now, obviously, I think that law is ridiculous and completely unfair, and I hope you do too—but back then, those were the rules.

So, back then, if you were *making up* a story about Jesus coming back to life, and if you wanted people to actually *believe* it, who would you say were the first witnesses to find Jesus alive again?

You would say they were men, right?

But that's *not* what we find in the biographies of Jesus.

Instead, on the morning of Jesus' resurrection, we find a group of *women* heading for the tomb where Jesus had been buried. When they get there, they find the tomb empty—and then Jesus himself meets them, and shows them that he's alive again (Matthew 28 v 5-10).

Now, I love this for a couple of reasons.

First, I love how Jesus looks at all the mistrust of women back then and goes, *Whatever, guys. I trust them. In fact, I'm going to show myself to* <u>*them*</u> *first.* Jesus has *zero* time for the idea that women are less reliable or less trustworthy witnesses than men.

But I also love it because it's another solid clue that Jesus' resurrection was a true historical event. Because, again, if Jesus' first followers were making it up, it's hard to imagine why they would have made it up like this.

There's way more to say about why we can trust that the disciples didn't just invent Jesus' resurrection, but for now, here's my point.

If you were one of Jesus' first followers, why on earth would you tell a story that made you look like such an idiot over and over again? Why would you celebrate your leader dying on a cross? Why would you even bother *trying* to convince people about a resurrection? And if you did, why, in that culture, would you claim that the first witnesses to that resurrection were women?

Unless, of course, those stories were true.

Unless you were committed to telling the whole truth about Jesus, no matter how embarrassing it was for you personally.

Unless you knew that the resurrection of Jesus had *actually happened.*

Chapter 5

DO JESUS' BIOGRAPHIES MATCH UP WITH THE REST OF HISTORY?

Let's say I tell you a story about the time, back in my first year of high school, when I accidentally dropped my iPhone on the train tracks on my way home from school.

It might sound believable enough, but a quick bit of investigating will tell you that this story isn't entirely true.

Why? Because my first year of high school was 1997—ten years before the iPhone was even invented.

So maybe the whole story is made up. Or maybe the story is *mostly* true, except for the detail about which brand of phone I had back then. But either way, the story doesn't quite check out—because it doesn't match up with what we already know about history.

But what if I tell you a story about the day in high school when I finally beat my friend's high score on Snake II on my old Nokia 3310?

Well, that's a more believable story, because that phone really *was* around when I was in high school, and it really *did* come with a game called Snake II.

The reason I bring this up isn't just to show you what an old man I am. It's because this kind of fact-checking is another way we can test the reliability of a historical source. The more the details of a text match up with the other historical information we already have, the more seriously we can take that text.

So what happens when we apply this test to the Bible?

△ △△△ △△△△ △

After spending a couple of pages describing Jesus' birth and childhood, Luke's Gospel fast-forwards to when Jesus was about 30 years old.

Luke kicks off this new section of his biography with this paragraph:

> *In the fifteenth year of the reign of Tiberius Caesar—when Pontius Pilate was governor of Judea, Herod tetrarch of Galilee, his brother Philip tetrarch of Iturea and Traconitis, and Lysanias tetrarch of Abilene—during the high-priesthood of Annas and Caiaphas, the word of God came to John son of Zechariah in the wilderness. He went into all the country around the*

Jordan, preaching a baptism of repentance for the forgiveness of sins. (Luke 3 v 1-3)

Not exactly page-turning stuff, is it?

This is the kind of paragraph you might be tempted to just skip over when you're reading the Bible—but the truth is, Luke is making a really important point.

By listing out all these *other* well-known people who lived at the same time as Jesus, and the areas they were in charge of, Luke is pinpointing the exact place and time that Jesus lived.

These days, if we want to list the year an event took place, we can just put a number on it.

Human beings first landed on the moon in AD 1969.

I wrote this book in AD 2020.

But back before the BC/AD calendar was invented, you couldn't just write down a number to explain when something happened. Instead, a common way of dating a historical event was to say, "In the [whatever number year] of the reign of [whichever king was around at the time]".

And that's exactly what Luke does here.

When did John the Baptist begin announcing to the people of Israel that the king they'd been waiting for was on the way? When did Jesus first arrive on the scene in public?

Not, "Once upon a time..."

Not, "Long, long ago..."

But, "In the fifteenth year of the reign of Tiberius Caesar" (v 1).

And since we have evidence from other historical sources that Tiberius Caesar became emperor of Rome in September of the year AD 14, this allows us to place John the Baptist's arrival at right around AD 28.

Luke also names the leaders Rome had put in charge of different nearby regions—Pilate, Herod, Philip and Lysanias—and also the two Jewish high priests who were running things at the time—Annas and Caiaphas.

These are *real* people from *real* history.

And what Luke is saying here is, *So is Jesus.*

△△△△△△△△△

Let's look at a different example.

John, in his Gospel, writes about the time Jesus healed a paralysed man at a pool in Jerusalem, which he describes like this:

> *Now there is in Jerusalem near the Sheep Gate a pool, which in Aramaic is called Bethesda and which is surrounded by five covered colonnades. (John 5 v 2)*

For hundreds of years, as archaeologists explored the city of Jerusalem, they found no sign of this five-sided pool—and so many people assumed that John had just made it up. They said this was evidence that John's Gospel *wasn't* a reliable first-century document after all but that someone had written it much later.

But then, in the mid-19th century, a German archaeologist uncovered the ruins of a pool near the Sheep Gate which perfectly matched John's description. Turns out John *didn't* make it up after all.

Then there's the Pool of Siloam, another pool mentioned in John's Gospel (John 9 v 7). Again, this pool lay buried for centuries—but then, in 2004, some builders doing some digging work for a sewer stumbled across the exact pool that John described.

John didn't invent these places. They really existed. And the evidence was right there beneath people's feet the whole time, just waiting to be found.

There are countless other examples. And, obviously, none of these discoveries *prove* that every single detail in Jesus' biographies is true. But what they *do* show us is that those biographies match up extremely closely with the other historical information we already have—and this is another massive reason to trust that the writers of the New Testament give us information about Jesus that is solid and reliable.

Chapter 6

INVESTIGATING THE EMPTY TOMB

Let's recap what we've figured out so far. In order to decide that a story from ancient history is actually true, what kind of evidence would you want to see?

Well, first, you'd want to see the same claims repeated by multiple independent sources—and in the case of Jesus, that's exactly what we find: at least five independent sources *inside* the Bible, plus another ten or so ancient mentions *outside* the Bible.

Second, you'd want those claims to be *earlier* (as in, as close as possible to the original events) rather than *later*. And in the case of Jesus, that's exactly what we find. All of our New Testament sources were written within living memory of Jesus.

Third, it would also be helpful to find embarrassing details inside those sources—details the writers would have *avoided* including, unless they were true. And in the case of Jesus, that's exactly what we find: in story after story, Jesus' first followers look like total embarrassments.

Fourth, you'd want to check that the details of your historical sources matched up well with what we already know about history. And in the case of Jesus, that's exactly what we find. The Gospels are firmly connected to real history—and to this day, archaeologists are still digging up new evidence showing that the world of first-century Israel was just how the Bible describes it.

And when we put all of this together, it adds up to solid evidence that the New Testament accounts of Jesus' life aren't just myths or legends. They're genuine historical sources that provide us with reliable information about Jesus. Which means they're going to be extremely useful to us as we finally turn to our next important question.

Did Jesus really rise from the dead?

Because remember, if we want to be sure that Christianity is really true—that Jesus was who he said he was—*this* is the question it all comes down to. And to figure *that* out, we need to start at Jesus' tomb—the cave where he was buried.

Imagine you're one of Jerusalem's religious leaders, back at the time when Jesus was put to death on the cross. You were there when the Roman soldiers crucified Jesus. You saw Jesus die with your own eyes.

You also know where he was buried—because you know that, after Jesus' death, another member of the Council, a man named Joseph of Arimathea, went to Pontius Pilate, asked for Jesus' body and buried it in a tomb (Luke 23 v 50-56).

But now imagine that, a few days later, you start to hear these weird rumours going around—rumours that Jesus isn't dead anymore and that people have seen him alive again.

What would be the quickest way to prove that these rumours are false?

It would be easy, right? All you'd have to do was go to the tomb, get Jesus' dead body, and say, "See? He hasn't come back to life. We've got his body right here!"

Except that's not what happened.

On Friday night, Jesus was dead and buried.

But by Sunday morning, the tomb was empty.

Jesus' body was gone.

△△△△△△△△△

How do we know the tomb was really empty?

Well, first, we have multiple independent sources all claiming that Jesus' first followers visited his tomb and found that Jesus' body wasn't there (Mark 16 v 6, John 20 v 1-2, 1 Corinthians 15 v 3-5).

We also have evidence that Jerusalem's religious leaders tried to explain the empty tomb by accusing Jesus' disciples of breaking in and stealing his body (Matthew 28 v 11-15)—which they obviously wouldn't have needed to do unless the tomb was actually empty.

If Jesus' tomb *wasn't* empty, Jerusalem's leaders could have just pulled out his body and disproved the resurrection rumours right then and there. If the tomb *wasn't* empty, the resurrection story would never have gotten off the ground.

But it did get off the ground.

Because, just days after Jesus' burial, the tomb really *was* empty.

So how do we explain that?

△ △ △ △ △ △ △ △ △

Imagine you work at a morgue, looking after dead bodies. You arrive one morning to find the front door broken open and a body missing.

Hopefully, your first thought isn't, *Whoa! They must have come back to life!*

Because, obviously, there's a much simpler explanation: someone must have come in during the night and stolen the body.

A stolen body is way more likely than a resurrection.

So how do we know that's not what happened with Jesus? How do we know the disciples didn't just break in, steal his body, and then just *pretend* he was alive again, just like those religious leaders said?

Well, as we already saw in Chapter 4, we've got good reasons to believe that Jesus' first followers were being truthful when they shared the story of Jesus' life.

But even if Jesus' disciples *had* wanted to steal Jesus' body, Jerusalem's leaders had done everything they could to make that impossible.

The leaders who had Jesus killed knew he'd been talking about coming back to life again. Obviously, they thought that was impossible—but they *did* suspect the disciples might try to steal his body and fake a resurrection:

> *The next day, the one after Preparation Day, the chief priests and the Pharisees went to Pilate. "Sir," they said, "we remember that while he was still alive that deceiver [Jesus] said, 'After three days I will rise again.' So give the order for the tomb to be made secure until the third day. Otherwise, his disciples may come and steal the body and tell the people that he has been raised from the dead. This last deception will be worse than the first."*
>
> *"Take a guard," Pilate answered. "Go, make the tomb as secure as you know how." So they went and made the tomb secure by putting a seal on the stone and posting the guard. (Matthew 27 v 62-66)*

Jesus' tomb wasn't just closed up with a big stone. It was *sealed shut* and guarded by heavily-armed soldiers.

Not to mention the fact that Jesus' disciples weren't even brave enough to stick around and defend Jesus' *living* body, back when he was arrested. So why would they suddenly risk their lives to steal his *dead* body?

Jesus' disciples didn't move the body. This theory just doesn't make sense.

And yet, somehow, Jesus' tomb still wound up empty.

Of course, the empty tomb all by itself doesn't *prove* that Jesus came back to life. But, at the very least, it creates a mystery that can't just be explained away—especially when we turn to our next piece of evidence: the multiple eyewitnesses who reported seeing Jesus alive again after he died.

Chapter 7

INVESTIGATING THE TESTIMONY OF JESUS' *friends*

Let's say that instead of writing a book about the actual, true resurrection of Jesus, I decide to write a book about a fake resurrection at my school, that I just make up myself.

For some strange reason, my publisher refuses to print *The Totally Real Resurrection at My School That I Definitely Did Not Make Up*—so I decide to publish it online myself.

A week later, the principal of my school calls me into his office.

He tells me he's read the book—and he's not happy about it. He says he can't have his teachers spreading ridiculous lies about his school.

My boss gives me a choice: either I immediately admit I've been lying, take the book down from the internet and send out a public apology—or I lose my job.

What will I choose?

Clearly, if I have even half a brain, I'll say sorry and admit I was lying! Trying to trick people into believing my made-up story might have seemed like a fun idea at the time, but I can't afford to lose my job over it!

But let's say I don't have half a brain. I convince myself that my made-up resurrection book is my ticket to fame and fortune, and I let my boss fire me. I *keep* lying about it all, until eventually things get so out of hand that the police show up at my door. They tell me I need to either give it up and admit I've been lying or I'm going to prison.

Now what will I choose?

Well, at this point the choice is even more obvious, right?

This dumb lie is not worth going to jail for!

Or let's say I find myself in an even *worse* situation. Let's say it's not the police coming to my house but someone much more dangerous.

It's the middle of the night. I jolt awake in bed at the sound of a rock smashing through my bedroom window. When I take a closer look, I see that the rock has a note wrapped round it. I untie the note and find a single sentence scrawled across the page: *Admit you've been lying or you're dead.*

At this point, there's *no way* I'm keeping the lie going.

Because if my lie was going to benefit me in some way—if it was going to bring me money or power or whatever—then, sure, maybe I'd keep telling it.

But if all my lie was going to bring me was suffering and death, then why in the world would I hold onto it?

△ △ △ △ △ △ △ △ △

We've seen that many of the writers of the Bible knew Jesus for themselves. For example, take a look at what John, one of Jesus' earliest disciples, says about Jesus:

> *We saw him with our own eyes and touched him with our own hands. (1 John 1 v 1, NLT)*

And right from the beginning, John and others claimed that Jesus was alive again. Jesus' first disciples said they'd not only *seen* him, but heard him, and eaten with him, and talked to him after he came back to life (for example, John 21 v 12-13). They claimed to have had real, repeated, undeniable, first-hand encounters with the resurrected Jesus.

Which basically leaves us with two possibilities:

1. They were lying.

2. They were telling the truth.

And even though we might not know for sure if Jesus' first followers were lying or not, *they* knew for sure. *They* knew if they had really seen Jesus alive again.

So, let's look at the first possibility—that Jesus' resurrection is a lie invented by his first followers.

The obvious first question is, *Why would they bother?*

Why would they give up their whole lives to follow a man they *knew* was dead?

As we saw way back at the start of this book, Jesus' first followers insisted all along that if Jesus *hadn't* come back to life, that proved he was a fraud, and that following him would be absolutely pointless (1 Corinthians 15 v 14).

The disciples had no reason to pretend Jesus was alive again if he wasn't, and they had *extremely* good reasons *not* to pretend he was alive again.

Because, as we've already seen, the same religious leaders who killed Jesus in the first place were working very hard to stop the rumours that Jesus had come back to life—and that meant arresting and beating up and even killing anyone who said they were a follower of Jesus.

Sticking to the story of Jesus' resurrection didn't bring his first followers money or power or an easy life. It brought them pain and suffering and imprisonment and death.

And still, they never gave up their claim that Jesus had come back to life.

If Jesus' resurrection was a lie, they *knew* it was a lie—so why in the world would they hold onto it, when they had nothing to gain and everything to lose?

On the other hand, if Jesus' resurrection was true, they *knew* it was true—and suddenly, their behaviour makes perfect sense.

Why did Jesus' first followers dedicate their lives to announcing his death and resurrection? Because they were convinced that it was through Jesus' death and resurrection that God was welcoming everyone, everywhere to come home to eternal life with him. They knew this was the greatest news in the history of the universe, and it was worth sharing, no matter the cost.

And why didn't Jesus' first followers give up their story, even in the face of death? Because they knew death wasn't the end of Jesus' story—which meant that, if they stuck with him, it didn't have to be the end of *their* story either.

If the story of Jesus' resurrection was a lie, it should have been easily stomped out, right back at the beginning. Instead, it spread like wildfire through the ancient world—and 2,000 years later, it's still going strong.

Chapter 8

INVESTIGATING THE TESTIMONY OF JESUS' brothers AND ENEMIES

Picture your brother or sister. (Or, if you don't have one, picture a close friend you've grown up with.) You know their habits. You know what makes them happy, or sad, or frustrated. You could probably do a really good impression of them. You can think of plenty of important, memorable moments you've shared together—but, more than that, you've got countless little memories of the countless ordinary days you've spent together.

Ok. Now imagine your brother or sister (or whoever) suddenly starts going out in public, claiming to be the new queen or king of your country. And not just any queen or king! Imagine they start dropping not-so-subtle hints that they're *God*, here on earth in human form.

Would you believe them?

If you're anything like me, the answer is a massive, obvious, unquestionable *no*.

I mean, I'd find claims like that hard to believe if *anyone* made them—but if there's one person in the whole world that I'm absolutely *certain* isn't God, it's my sister.

It's not that she's a horrible person or anything. She's great.

But she's my *sister*.

For more than 30 years now, we've lived our completely ordinary, unremarkable lives together. Obviously, if she tried to convince me she was some kind of world-saving ruler or saviour or *God*, I'd say she was out of her mind!

And so it probably shouldn't surprise us that that's *exactly* what Jesus' brothers thought about him.

△ △△△ △△△ △△

After Jesus was born, his mother, Mary, and her husband, Joseph, had a bunch of other children. Jesus grew up in a village called Nazareth, surrounded by brothers and sisters.

The first time we meet Jesus' siblings in the Bible, Jesus is about 30 years old. He's just returned to Nazareth after spending some time travelling through the nearby villages, claiming that, through *him*, God has come to rescue his people.

> *Then Jesus entered a house, and again a crowd gathered, so that he and his disciples were not even able*

> *to eat. When his family heard about this, they went to take charge of him, for they said, "He is out of his mind."*
> *(Mark 3 v 20-21)*

When Jesus starts acting as if he's God's long-promised King, his family tries to pull him away from the crowd and talk some sense into him. They think he's gone crazy!

Which is about what you'd expect, right?

But fast-forward a few decades, and we find something you absolutely would *not* expect. It's a letter written by Jesus' brother James. In this letter, James introduces himself as "a servant of God and of the Lord Jesus Christ" (James 1 v 1), and then goes on to call Jesus "our glorious Lord" (2 v 1).

And a few years after that, we find a letter written by Jude, another one of Jesus' brothers. Jude also introduces himself as "a servant of Jesus Christ" (Jude v 1), and then goes on to describe Jesus as "our only Master and Lord" (v 4, ESV) and the one who can "bring you to eternal life" (v 21).

As much as I love my sister, there's no way I'm going to start calling her "our glorious Lord" anytime soon—but that's how Jesus' brothers describe him.

And here's what's even harder to explain: we've got absolutely zero evidence to suggest that Jesus' brothers followed him anytime before he died.

And so it's not just that Jesus' brothers changed their minds and decided that Jesus actually was the glorious

King of the universe. It's that they changed their minds *after* Jesus had already died!

Why?

What changed their minds?

Well, the Bible says that, for James at least, the answer was seeing his formerly-dead brother alive again in person (1 Corinthians 15 v 7).

And that's the only thing that would do it, right?

Think about the evidence you'd need to be convinced that your own brother or sister was God—because *whatever* evidence Jesus' brothers needed to flip from thinking he was crazy to worshipping him as King... they got it.

What else but a resurrection could explain that?

△ △ △ △ △ △ △ △ △

And Jesus' siblings weren't the only ones to start following Jesus after he died.

In the New Testament book of Acts we meet a man named Saul, who was part of a religious group called the Pharisees—the group responsible for arresting Jesus and convincing Pontius Pilate to have him killed.

Saul became obsessed with silencing *anyone* who said that Jesus had risen from the dead. He set out on a mission to track down Jesus' followers and have them arrested and even killed.

If changing Jesus' brothers' minds about Jesus was a massive challenge, changing *Saul's* mind was impossible. It would *never* happen!

Well, I mean, until it did.

If you open the New Testament of your Bible, you'll find *13* letters written by Saul (or, as he was known by that point, Paul), shouting the praises of the resurrected Jesus.

Almost overnight, he went from throwing people into prison for worshipping Jesus to getting thrown into prison for worshipping Jesus himself. He dedicated the rest of his life to announcing the news that Jesus was alive.

And again we need to ask ourselves the question, *What in the world could have changed his mind?*

Well, according to Paul, it's because he *met* the risen Jesus (1 Corinthians 15 v 8)—and it turns out it's way harder to believe someone's dead when you're having a conversation with them.

△ △ △ △ △ △ △ △ △

And so, as we search for the truth about Jesus' resurrection, it's not just the behaviour of Jesus' original disciples that we need to explain—the ones who were already following him before he died.

We also need to explain why these people who were completely set *against* believing that Jesus was who he claimed to be, suddenly flipped and started following him *after he'd already been killed.*

And in case you're thinking, *Yeah, but that's still a pretty small group of people; it could still all just be made up*, we've got one more set of eyewitnesses to check in with.

And this time, it's not a small group.

This time, there are 500 of them.

Chapter 9

INVESTIGATING THE 500 OTHER EYEWITNESSES

Let's go back to that imaginary situation where I decide to write a book about a fake resurrection at my school.

Obviously, no matter what I did, this would be an extremely difficult claim to get you to believe. And if I wanted to have any chance of convincing you, there's one thing I'd absolutely *have* to do: keep you away from everyone else at my school.

Because as soon as you called the office, or emailed my principal, or talked to one of the other teachers, or to anyone who actually went to my school, they'd give you the same answer: "What are you talking about? That never happened. He just made it all up."

As soon as you talked to the people who were actually around at the time this so-called resurrection was meant to have happened, my whole story would fall apart.

And so if I wanted to have *any* hope of convincing you about a lie like that, the absolute dumbest thing I could possibly say would be, "Ask anyone! They all saw it!"

Because they *didn't* all see it.

And the more of them you spoke to, the more obvious it would be that I'd made the whole thing up.

On the other hand, if a *real* resurrection took place, and if hundreds of people *did* see this dead person alive again, going and talking to some of those people would be a fantastic way to confirm that the story was true.

If, for example, we could talk to 500 different people who'd all seen Jesus alive again with their own eyes, that would be a massive game-changer in our quest to figure out if Jesus' resurrection was a real historical event.

Wouldn't it be amazing if we had access to that kind of evidence?

Well, the good news is, we kind of do.

Sometime between the years AD 53 and AD 57, Paul wrote a letter to a group of Christians in the city of Corinth in Greece.

Towards the end of this letter, Paul outlined the key details of the Jesus message. If the Corinthians wanted to know the most basic facts about the good news of Jesus, Paul said, here's what they needed to know:

- Jesus died in our place to pay the price for all the ways we've made a mess of our relationships with God, just like God promised he would (1 Corinthians 15 v 3).
- Jesus came back to life on the third day, just like God promised he would (v 4).
- Jesus appeared to Cephas (aka Peter) and the rest of his twelve disciples, showing them that he was alive (v 5).
- Jesus appeared alive again to over *500* other witnesses at the same time (v 6).

And then Paul dropped in this detail: *Some of those 500 witnesses have died by now, but most of them are still alive* (v 6).

Why did Paul say this?

He was inviting the Corinthians to go and fact-check his story.

He was saying, *I'm not just making this up. They all saw Jesus alive again too. If you don't believe me, go check with them. Ask anyone! They all saw it!*

Now, obviously, we can't go and talk to those eyewitnesses. It's been nearly 2,000 years since Paul wrote his letter to the Corinthians, and all 500 of them are well and truly dead by now.

But the original readers of this letter *could* go and ask.

If they weren't convinced about Paul's claim that Jesus had risen from the dead, they could go find one of these witnesses, knock on their door and ask them if Paul was telling the truth.

And if they still weren't sure, they could go knock on another door and ask another person.

And another.

And another.

They could keep knocking on doors, and questioning eyewitnesses, and fact-checking Paul's story, over and over and over again, until they were convinced Paul really was telling the truth.

△△△△△△△△△

But, you may be wondering, how does that help us?

I mean, sure, that's great for those first-century readers, back in Corinth.

But what good is that to us, here in the twenty-first century, long after all those witnesses have died?

Well, like I said back at the beginning of the chapter, if I was trying to convince you about a *fake* resurrection, the absolute dumbest thing I could say would be, "Ask anyone! They all saw it!"

Because when you did go and ask, you'd figure out pretty quickly that I'd made the whole thing up.

But this is *exactly* the strategy Paul chose!

He was *so confident* in his claim that Jesus rose from the dead, that he invited the Corinthians to go ask around and confirm it for themselves.

And here's the thing: if Paul was lying about Jesus' resurrection, the Corinthians would have *realised* it was a lie as soon as they started asking around. And once they figured out that Paul was lying, they would've thrown his letter in the garbage, given up following Jesus, and gone on with their lives.

But that's not what happened.

Instead, Paul's original readers thought his letters were *so important* that they copied them out again and again—which is how *we've* still got access to them, nearly 2,000 years later.

And the most logical explanation for this is that Paul was telling the truth—that when his readers went out to fact-check his story, they found eyewitness after eyewitness who said, "Yeah, I know it might sound crazy—but it's true. Jesus didn't stay dead. He's alive again. I saw it with my own eyes."

Chapter 10

INVESTIGATING THE EXPLOSIVE GROWTH OF THE CHURCH

How much do you know about a man named Simon of Peraea?

What about Judas the Galilean? (Not the famous Judas Iscariot who betrayed Jesus; I'm talking about the first-century rebel leader.)

What about a guy called Theudas?

Unless you're *massively* into first-century Jewish history, I'm guessing you've never even *heard* of these men.

Which is interesting—because they all have quite a bit in common with Jesus.

See, Jesus wasn't the only person of his time who went around claiming to be a new king. The Jewish people *hated* that the Roman Empire had invaded their land and put themselves in charge. So they were waiting for a saviour—the one they called the *Messiah*—the rescuing king they believed God had promised would come and set them free.

And there were *plenty* of people waiting in line to put their hand up for the job. Jesus was just one of a whole *bunch* of teachers and leaders who showed up, saying, "Follow me! I'm going to rescue our people!"

So how come Jesus is the only one you've heard of?

To answer that question, let's take a closer look at some of these other would-be kings...

△ △△△ △△△△ △

According to Josephus, Simon of Peraea was once a slave of Herod the Great—the king who the Romans had put in charge of Israel. But then, when Herod died, Simon declared *himself* to be the new king. He got himself a crown, gathered a bunch of followers, and burned down the royal palace at Jericho, along with a bunch of Herod's other houses. But then Gratus, Herod's army commander, chased Simon down and cut off his head—and all Simon's followers ran off and disappeared.

Simon of Peraea's rebellion died with him.

At around the same time, after the Roman Empire raised the taxes it collected from the Jewish people, Judas the Galilean decided that enough was enough. He pulled together a crew of followers and led a violent rebellion against Rome. Unfortunately for Judas, Rome hit back just as violently. They killed Judas and a bunch of his followers, and the ones who were left ran off and disappeared.

Judas the Galilean's rebellion died with him.

Then there's Theudas. Actually, there were most likely two guys called Theudas who led two *different* rebellions.

The first Theudas came onto the scene *before* Judas the Galilean. He gathered around 400 followers before getting killed by the Romans.

The second Theudas arrived *after* Judas the Galilean. He claimed to have been sent by God himself to free his people from the Romans—a claim that fell apart a bit when a troop of Roman horsemen chased him down and chopped off his head.

And both times, after these guys were killed, their surviving followers ran off, and both of their rebellions died with them—because who in their right mind would keep putting their hope in a dead leader?

Over and over again, we see the same pattern:

1. A leader shows up and says, "Follow me! I'm going to rescue our people!"
2. The leader gathers a crowd of excited followers.
3. The leader gets killed by the Romans.
4. Their followers run away and hide.
5. The leader's movement dies out and gets forgotten.

And so it makes perfect sense that you've never heard of any of these guys. They're a bunch of 2,000-year-old rebels from a tiny corner of the Roman Empire who *failed* at the only thing that might have made them famous!

But then we come to Jesus:

1. Jesus showed up and said, "Follow me! I'm going to rescue our people!"

2. He gathered a crowd of excited followers.

3. He got killed by the Romans.

4. His followers ran away and hid.

And then... something completely weird happened.

A few days after Jesus' death, his followers were back together again. And, instead of dying out and getting forgotten like every other movement, the Jesus movement started *getting bigger*. Almost overnight, it gathered *thousands* of new followers.

And even though both the Roman Empire *and* the Jewish religious leaders did everything they could to stamp the Jesus message out—even though Jesus' followers were regularly beaten up and put in prison and even *killed* for following him—the Jesus movement just kept on growing.

How do we explain that?

△ △△△ △△△△△

Not long after Jesus died (and, according to his followers, rose to life and returned to heaven), a teacher named Gamaliel said something that I think makes a lot of sense.

Luke records a scene in the book of Acts where Gamaliel and a bunch of other Jewish religious leaders are discussing what to do with Jesus' first disciples, and with this claim they were spreading about Jesus coming back to life.

During the conversation, Gamaliel gets up and says this...

> *Some time ago Theudas appeared, claiming to be somebody, and about four hundred men rallied to him. He was killed, all his followers were dispersed, and it all came to nothing. After him, Judas the Galilean appeared in the days of the census and led a band of people in revolt. He too was killed, and all his followers were scattered. Therefore, in the present case I advise you: leave these men alone! Let them go! For if their purpose or activity is of human origin, it will fail. But if it is from God, you will not be able to stop these men; you will only find yourselves fighting against God.*
> *(Acts 5 v 36-39)*

If the resurrection of Jesus is made up, Gamaliel says, *if Jesus is just another false Messiah—just another dead rebel leader like Theudas and Judas and all the others—then his followers will fade away, just like all theirs did.*

But if Jesus really did come back to life—if he truly is the Messiah—then this movement he's started is going to be absolutely unstoppable.

And it was.

And so the question is, if Jesus *didn't* come back to life, then why in the world did his followers keep following him? Why have you even heard of him at all?

Well, you're going to need to figure out your own answer to that question.

But if you ask me, the answer that makes the most sense of the evidence is that Gamaliel was right—that he was even *more* right than he knew. If you ask me, the most logical reason that Jesus' message didn't die with him is that Jesus didn't stay dead.

Chapter 11

If it's true... WHAT SHOULD I DO?

When you actually take the time to investigate the claim that Jesus rose from the dead, it brings up a whole bunch of pretty huge questions.

Like, if Jesus *didn't* come back to life...

How did his heavily-guarded tomb suddenly become empty?

Why did Jesus' closest friends all claim they'd seen Jesus alive again? And why on earth did they all stick to that story, even when it meant getting beaten up and thrown into prison and even killed?

Why did Jesus' brothers—who, before Jesus died, all thought he was crazy—suddenly change their minds *after* Jesus died and start worshipping their own brother as the risen King of the universe?

What made Paul suddenly switch from violently attacking Jesus' first followers to *joining* Jesus' first followers and dedicating his life to the claim that Jesus was alive? And what about those *500* other eyewitnesses that Paul invited his readers to go and chat to?

And if *every other leader* who claimed to be God's promised Messiah was abandoned by their followers as soon as they were killed by the Romans, why did the complete *opposite* happen to Jesus?

We have reliable historical evidence for all these events—and so the question is, *What's the best way to explain them?*

If Jesus' resurrection didn't happen, none of it seems to make much sense.

But if a resurrection *did* happen, this is exactly the kind of historical evidence you'd expect it to leave behind.

"But," you may be wondering, "if the evidence for Jesus' resurrection is really as strong as you say it is, why doesn't *everyone* believe it? Why are there still so many people who think it never happened?"

It's a great question—and I think the answer is different for different people.

First off, I've met plenty of people who say, "I don't believe in the resurrection because there's not enough evidence"—but quite often, the truth is they haven't actually spent much time looking into it. They're just *assuming* there's not much evidence rather than actually taking the time to find out.

Maybe that was you before you started this book. If it was, I hope I've been able to show you that there are way better reasons to believe in Jesus' resurrection than you thought there were.

△△△△△△△△△

Then there are other people who say, "I don't care *how* much evidence you think you have, there must be another explanation, because dead people *can't* come back to life again. That would be a *miracle* and science says miracles aren't real."

But actually, science doesn't say that at all.

What science does tell us is how the universe *usually* works. We observe the world around us, and we run experiments, and we figure out, a bit at a time, the way our universe is put together.

Science is our *best* tool for figuring out the normal rules of the universe.

Rules like, *Dead people stay dead.*

And when the Bible talks about miracles, it's not arguing with *any* of that.

It's saying, *Yeah, of course those rules are true! That's how God set things up when he created the universe in the first place! But since God's the one who invented the normal rules of the universe, he can step in and break them anytime he wants.*

If you're willing to keep an open mind about God, then it makes perfect sense to keep an open mind about miracles too.

△△△△△△△△△

But I think there's a third reason why some people deny the resurrection.

They might not admit it's their actual reason. They might not even *realise* it. More likely, they'll point to one of the other reasons we've already talked about. But I honestly think that, deep down, some people just don't *want* Jesus' resurrection to be true.

Because, like I said way back at the beginning of this book, Jesus claimed to be so much more than just another leader or king—he made claims about himself that only *God* could truly make.

Jesus claimed that every single one of us has broken our relationship with God, and that only *he* could make things right again. Jesus claimed that, through his death and resurrection, he was making a way for anyone who puts their trust in him to come back home to God. Jesus claimed to be our *only hope* for an eternal life that lasts forever.

And if Jesus really *did* rise from the dead, those aren't just claims. They're true.

Which means the truth of the resurrection isn't just a *historical* question.

It's a *personal* question.

Because if the resurrection is true, it should transform our whole lives. If Jesus *really* came back to life, then he's our one true God and King and *everybody* should follow him. Which means handing over control of our lives and letting Jesus be in charge.

And not everybody wants to put Jesus in charge.

A little while back, this pastor I know started meeting up each week with a friend of his so they could read the Bible together. But then one day, his friend said he wanted to stop.

The pastor wondered if maybe he'd said something to offend his friend, or if his friend was getting bored, or if he'd just decided the Bible wasn't true.

But the friend said, no, it wasn't that he'd decided Jesus' resurrection couldn't be true. It was actually the opposite: the more he investigated, the more convinced he became that the resurrection *was* true.

Which would mean Jesus really was who he said he was.

Which would mean the only sensible response would be to turn around and follow him.

And this guy didn't want to do that.

So he just walked away from the whole thing.

But maybe *that's* not you either.

Maybe this book has shown you that there's more evidence for the resurrection than you thought—and maybe you're open to it being true, but you're still not quite convinced yet. Maybe you're honestly trying to figure all this out, and you want to know the truth, but you still have heaps of questions and doubts.

That's great! Questions and doubts aren't bad at all. They show that we're still learning and growing and figuring stuff out.

And the good news is that there's *way* more to learn about the life, death, and resurrection of Jesus than I've had space for in this little book. There are whole piles of other evidence that I haven't even had space to mention.

But the truth is, evidence by itself isn't going to change our minds. Because, like I said, this isn't just a historical question. It's personal—partly because of the stuff I said before, and partly because *Jesus himself* is a person. And the truth is, the only way you're ever really going to be convinced about him is if you try getting to know him for yourself—which, if he really is alive, you'll soon find out is absolutely possible!

Try reading the biographies of Jesus in the Bible. (If you've never done this before, I'd suggest starting with the Gospel of Mark—and if you need a hand making sense of it, I've written another book called *Best News Ever* to take you through it step-by-step.)

Try making prayer a regular part of your routine. Ask Jesus to help you keep on figuring out who he is.

If you have friends or people in your family who follow Jesus, ask them why *they* believe this stuff. And if you're not already part of a church community, then joining one is a great thing to do—because getting to know Jesus is way easier and more rewarding when you have other people on the journey with you.

And if you're already doing all that... great! I hope this book has given you even more reason to keep putting your trust in Jesus, and I hope it's made you even more confident and excited to tell other people the reason for the amazing hope you have in him. You might even like to pass this book on to a friend and share the good news with them that way!

And whoever you are, and wherever you're up to with all this stuff, don't stop exploring.

Because the message of Christianity is not just *true*—it's the greatest news in all of history! And as you keep investigating, keep asking questions, keep getting to know Jesus, you'll discover that he's more than just *alive*. He's strong and kind and he loves you more than you can possibly imagine—and life with *him* is the richest, fullest, best life imaginable.

References

The funny thing about writing a book about ancient history is that, if you do your job right, very few of your ideas are original. That's certainly the case with this book. Over the past 20 years or so, my investigation of Jesus has been helped along by all kinds of great authors and teachers in all kinds of situations—far too many to possibly list here—but these people in particular deserve special mention:

Back when I was in high school and I started exploring all this evidence-for-Jesus stuff for myself, three books that I found incredibly helpful were *The Case for Christ* by Lee Strobel, *Who Moved the Stone?* by Frank Morison, and *A Hell of A Life* by John Dickson. These authors helped me to understand in a profound new way that the Bible's claims about Jesus are backed up by solid historical evidence. The truths from those books have been rattling around in my brain ever since, and I'm sure many of them have now made it into this book in one way or another.

In 2013, I had the privilege of travelling through Israel/ Palestine and visiting many of the ancient sites I talk about in this book. My tour guides on that trip were John Dickson and Stephen Langfur, who loaded my brain up with countless insights into how ancient historians view the Bible, which have been immensely valuable in the writing of this book.

My description of what the Bible means when it talks about "faith" owes a lot to an incredibly helpful talk that Amy Orr-Ewing presented at my school a couple of years back.

The massive difference between other teachers saying, "Here is the way," and Jesus saying, "I am the way," was something I first picked up in a sermon by Timothy Keller, and the idea that the point of Luke 3 v 1-3 is to locate Jesus in real history is something I first heard in a sermon by Jeff Manion.

And finally, Richard Bauckham has written a (gigantic) book called *Jesus and the Eyewitnesses*, which helped me understand and explain why the New Testament accounts of Jesus' life couldn't be just myths that developed over time.

Thank yous

Thanks to Rachel Jones for being such an insightful and patient editor, to André Parker for his awesome design, to Emma Randall for the fantastic illustrations and cover artwork, and to the whole team at TGBC for getting behind this series and helping it to be the best it can be.

Huge thanks to Hannah Chalmers, Micah Ford, Corlette Graham, Ella and Fran Jewell, Hannah, Grace, and Georgie Moodie, and Sophia Tollitt, for reading early drafts of this book. Your insights and encouragement have been incredibly helpful.

Thanks to the staff, students and families of PLC Sydney. It is one of the great privileges of my life to share the good news of Jesus with you every week. In particular, thanks to my 2020 Year 5 classes—5B, 5E, 5O, and 5W—who heard these books first, and provided heaps of useful feedback.

Thanks to Mum and Dad for the countless hours you've poured into talking through my big questions about God over the past 30+ years.

Thanks to Katie and Waz, Phil and Meredith, and Kerryn and Andrew, for your constant love, support, wisdom, and encouragement.

Thanks to Hattie, for helping me see the love of God more clearly. May you grow up full of big questions, and may you keep turning back to our great king Jesus for the answers.

Thanks to Tom French for being a brilliant writing and podcasting buddy.

Thanks to Rowan McAuley for your friendship and partnership in the gospel, and for being so constantly enthusiastic and encouraging about these books, even though they keep dragging me away from the novels we're meant to be writing.

Last but not least, thanks to my church family at Abbotsford Presbyterian. In particular, a huge shout-out to the whole crew at YCentral—may this book help you to see even more clearly the abundant love God has for you in Jesus.

Keep asking big questions:

Big Questions is a series of fun and fast-paced books walking you through what the Bible says about some of the big questions of life, helping you to grow in confident and considered faith.

thegoodbook.co.uk/big-questions
thegoodbook.com/big-questions
thegoodbook.com.au/big-questions

Also by Chris Morphew:

A devotional 100-day journey through Mark's fast-paced, action-packed story—bringing you face to face with Jesus: the one who changes everything.

thegoodbook.co.uk/best-news-ever
thegoodbook.com/best-news-ever
thegoodbook.com.au/best-news-ever

thegoodbook
COMPANY

BIBLICAL | RELEVANT | ACCESSIBLE

At The Good Book Company, we are dedicated to helping Christians and local churches grow. We believe that God's growth process always starts with hearing clearly what he has said to us through his timeless word—the Bible.

Ever since we opened our doors in 1991, we have been striving to produce Bible-based resources that bring glory to God. We have grown to become an international provider of user-friendly resources to the Christian community, with believers of all backgrounds and denominations using our books, Bible studies, devotionals, evangelistic resources, and DVD-based courses.

We want to equip ordinary Christians to live for Christ day by day, and churches to grow in their knowledge of God, their love for one another, and the effectiveness of their outreach.

Call us for a discussion of your needs or visit one of our local websites for more information on the resources and services we provide.

Your friends at The Good Book Company